APEX PREDATORS
of the Amazon Rain Forest

Bull Shark

by Ellen Lawrence

Consultant:

John Richardson
Conservation Officer, The Shark Trust
Plymouth, United Kingdom

BEARPORT
PUBLISHING

New York, New York

Credits
Cover, © Pete Oxford/Minden Pictures/FLPA, © orlandin/Shutterstock, and © Rich Carey/Shutterstock; 4, © Amazon-Images/Alamy; 5, © Mark Conlin/Alamy; 6, © Premium UIG/Getty Images; 7, © Doug Perrine/Alamy; 8, © Cosmographics; 9, © Pete Oxford/Minden Pictures/FLPA; 10T, © Dr. Morley Read/Shutterstock; 10B, © Ben Horton/Getty Images; 11, © Terry Moore/Stocktrek Images/Alamy; 12, © Michael Patrick O'Neill/Alamy; 13, © Arco Images GmbH/Alamy and © HamsterMan/Shutterstock; 14, © Jani Oravisjärvi; 15, © Reuters/Alamy; 16, © Michael Patrick O'Neill/Alamy; 17, © Bryan Clark/Deeper Blue; 18–19, © wildestanimal/Getty Images; 20, © Jeff Rotman/Alamy; 21, © Michael Patrick O'Neill/Alamy; 22, © Ruby Tuesday Books; 23TL, © Doug Perrine/Alamy; 23TC, © Michael Patrick O'Neill/Alamy; 23TR, © Stefan Pircher/Shutterstock; 23BL, © FloridaStock/Shutterstock; 23BC, © Reuters/Alamy; 23BR, © Fotos593/Shutterstock.

Publisher: Kenn Goin
Editor: Jessica Rudolph
Creative Director: Spencer Brinker
Photo Researcher: Ruby Tuesday Books Ltd

Library of Congress Cataloging-in-Publication Data

Names: Lawrence, Ellen, 1967– , author.
Title: Bull shark / by Ellen Lawrence.
Description: New York, NY : Bearport Publishing, 2017. | Series: Apex
   predators of the Amazon rain forest | Includes bibliographical references
   and index. | Audience: Ages 5 to 8.
Identifiers: LCCN 2016043978 (print) | LCCN 2016048678 (ebook) | ISBN
   9781684020355 (library) | ISBN 9781684020874 (ebook)
Subjects: LCSH: Bull shark—Juvenile literature.
Classification: LCC QL638.95.C3 L39 2017 (print) | LCC QL638.95.C3 (ebook) |
   DDC 597.3/4—dc23
LC record available at https://lccn.loc.gov/2016043978

For more information, write to Bearport Publishing Company, Inc., 45 West 21st Street, Suite 3B, New York, New York 10010. Printed in the United States of America.

10 9 8 7 6 5 4 3 2 1

Contents

Danger in the River

It's early evening in the Amazon **rain forest**.

A turtle is slowly swimming in a river.

Suddenly, something bumps the animal, then . . . *crunch*!

The turtle disappears into a giant mouth filled with sharp teeth.

What huge **predator** is hunting in the river?

It's a powerful bull shark!

turtle

Most sharks live in oceans. Bull sharks, however, make their homes in oceans and in rivers.

bull shark

Meet a Bull Shark

Bull sharks have large, solid bodies and rounded snouts.

Adult bull sharks weigh about 300 to 500 pounds (136 to 227 kg).

The male sharks usually grow to be 8 feet (2.4 m) long from snout to tail.

Females are larger and can grow to be 11 feet (3.4 m) long!

snout

dorsal fin

A shark has a dorsal **fin** on its back for balance. This fin stops the animal from tipping over to one side. It also has a fin on each side of its body to help it steer. Its tail fin helps push it through the water.

tail fin

fin for steering

adult bull shark

A Bull Shark's World

Bull sharks live in shallow water mostly in tropical, or very warm, parts of the world.

They can survive in both salty oceans and freshwater rivers, such as the Amazon River.

They often make their homes near the shore or in areas where a river flows into an ocean.

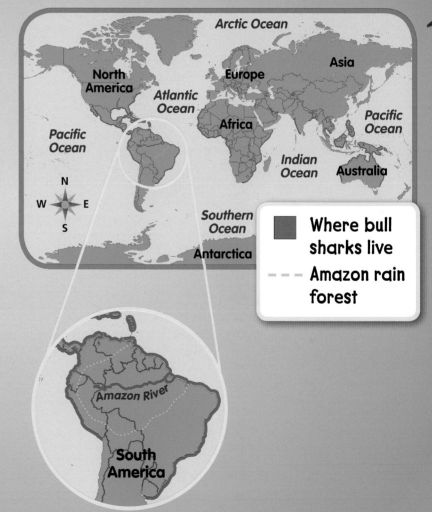

Arctic Ocean

North America

Europe

Asia

Atlantic Ocean

Africa

Pacific Ocean

Pacific Ocean

Indian Ocean

Australia

Southern Ocean

Antarctica

N
W · E
S

Where bull sharks live

--- Amazon rain forest

Amazon River

South America

a bull shark swimming close to shore

A bull shark spends most of its time swimming slowly. If it spots a meal, however, it can swim very fast, covering a distance of 100 feet (30 m) in just five seconds!

Bull sharks often hunt in dark, muddy rivers. How do you think they find animals to eat?

Out of Sight

The rivers that flow through the Amazon rain forest can be very murky.

The water may be so cloudy that a bull shark can't see the **prey** it hunts.

However, the shark has a powerful sense of smell.

The skillfull hunter uses its nostrils to detect prey in the water.

a muddy river in the Amazon rain forest

a bull shark in murky water

snout

pores

nostril

A bull shark can
also detect prey using
tiny pores, or holes, on its
body. These pores pick up
weak electrical signals that
all animals produce.

Bump and Bite!

The way a bull shark attacks its prey is known as "bump and bite."

When a bull shark finds an animal, it bumps the creature with its snout.

This helps the shark determine if the animal is something it wants to eat.

If the animal is prey, the shark then swallows it whole or bites off chunks of it.

a shark eating the head of a fish

A bull shark may lose some teeth while tearing at its prey. This isn't a problem for the hunter, though. Why do you think this is?

piranha

In the Amazon and other rivers, bull sharks hunt for turtles, fish, and waterbirds such as herons. They may even feed on deer, cattle, and other large animals that enter the water to take a drink.

heron

Hundreds of Teeth

A bull shark has the most powerful bite of any type of shark.

Inside its mouth are rows filled with hundreds of very sharp teeth.

The front row of teeth is for biting and tearing food.

Behind the front teeth are rows of **replacement** teeth.

If a shark loses a tooth, a replacement tooth gradually moves forward to fill in the gap!

a bull shark tooth

serrations

The edges of a bull shark's teeth have jagged edges for tearing flesh. These tiny razor-sharp points are called serrations.

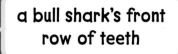

a bull shark's front row of teeth

a replacement tooth moving forward

rows of replacement teeth

15

Young Predators

Adult bull sharks meet up around once a year to **mate**.

About 11 months after mating, the female shark gives birth in a shallow river.

Her babies are called pups.

As soon as they are born, the shark pups are able to swim and take care of themselves.

The fierce little predators hunt for fish, water rats, and other small prey.

a pair of bull sharks

Why do you think a female shark gives birth to her pups in a river and not in an ocean?

baby bull shark

A mother shark can give birth to up to 13 pups at one time. A newborn pup is about 29 inches (74 cm) long.

Growing Up

A bull shark pup spends the first few years of its life in the safety of a river.

Out at sea, it might become a meal for a tiger shark or other large shark.

The only predator that might eat a pup in a river is an adult bull shark.

By the time a young bull shark is four years old, it's about 5 feet (1.5 m) long.

Now it's big enough to survive in the ocean.

If a bull shark is attacked by another shark, it will throw up everything in its stomach. The attacker then starts feeding on the vomit, and the bull shark can try to escape!

a researcher feeding a young bull shark in the ocean

How do you think the bull shark got its name?

An Apex Predator

Once it's an adult, a bull shark has few predators.

Out at sea, a bull shark might be attacked by a bigger shark, such as a great white.

In a river like the Amazon, however, bull sharks are apex predators.

This means the sharks eat many of the animals that share their home—but nothing eats them!

This blacktip reef shark was partly eaten by a bull shark.

Bull sharks got their name because they are heavy and stocky like bulls. They also bump, or butt, their prey, just like bulls that butt each other with their heads.

a bull shark eating a fish

21

Science Lab

An Amazon River Food Chain

The Amazon River is home to many different plants and animals. All these living things need food for energy. A food chain shows how the plants and animals get their food. For example:

| Water plants make food using sunlight. | → | A shrimp eats water plants. | → | A fish eats the shrimp. | → | A bull shark eats the fish. |

You will need:
- Styrofoam cups
- Colored markers

In a library or online, research the different animals that bull sharks eat and what their prey eat. Make an Amazon food chain using cups. Draw and label the plants and animals on the cups.

Plant

Shrimp

Fish

Bull Shark

Bull Shark

Fish

Shrimp

Plant

Present your cups to friends and family to explain your Amazon River food chain. Stack the cups to show that a bull shark is the apex predator because nothing eats the shark.

Science Words

fin (FIN) a flat part of a shark's or fish's body that is used for swimming

mate (MAYT) to come together in order to have young

predator (PRED-uh-tur) an animal that hunts other animals for food

prey (PRAY) an animal that is hunted and eaten by another animal

rain forest (RAYN FORE-ist) a large area of land covered with trees and other plants where lots of rain falls

replacement (rih-PLAYSS-ment) a thing that takes the place of another, such as a new tooth

Index

Read More

Gerstein, Sherry. *Sharks (See-Thru Books).* Minneapolis, MN: Millbrook (2015).

Hopper, Whitney. *In Search of Bull Sharks (Shark Search).* New York: PowerKids Press (2016).

Rake, Jody S. *Bull Shark (Shark Zone).* North Mankato, MN: Capstone (2011).

Learn More Online

To learn more about bull sharks, visit
www.bearportpublishing.com/ApexPredators

About the Author

Ellen Lawrence lives in the United Kingdom. Her favorite books to write are those about nature and animals. In fact, the first book Ellen bought for herself, when she was six years old, was the story of a gorilla named Patty Cake that was born in New York's Central Park Zoo.